ROCK painting

Jaclyn Crupi

hinkler

About This Book

This book contains everything you need to know to create beautiful and unique rock paintings.

To make great rock paintings you will need:

- Rocks of various shapes and sizes
- Paints (you will need all primary colors plus black and white)
- Paint brushes with both flat and round bristles
- Chalk
- Paint mixing tray
- Old jar (for water for your brushes)
- Felt
- Pencil
- Masking tape
- Sticky tape
- Old newspaper
- Large bull clip
- Paint pens
- Felt-tip pen

Cover photography © Susan Miller http://www.SusanMillerIllustrator.com
Owl, mouse, ladybug, gnome and cat rocks painted by Helen O'Dare
Images © Shutterstock.com: Paint and brushes © Aprilphoto; Stones © nrt; Cave painting © Pichugin Dmitry; Hand style cave painting © Eduardo Rivero; Cave painting © edella; Cave painting © Viktoriya Field; Cave painting © pedrosala; Cave painting © ThavornC; Pebbles © strelov; Six rocks © Iwona Grodzka; River rocks © James Wheeler; Black pebbles © Scorpp; Black and white pebbles © discpicture; Hand with paint and brushes, Paint and brushes, Pizza © Africa Studio; Paint and brushes © Denphumi; Bull clip © photosync; Girl painting © Max Topchii; Boy drawing © Jeka; Paintbrushes © Jiri Hera; Pots of paint and brushes © straga; Ladybug © Matej Ziak; Tortoise © fivespots; Clown fish © val lawless; Coral © antos777; Caterpillar © Tomas1111; Butterfly © suns07; Bee © Serg64; Owl © Eric Isselee; Panda © kidy; Eyes © blojfo; Ghost faces © Alekksall; Pumpkins © My Lit'l Eye; Pumpkin faces © MarketOlya; Spider © Jacob Hamblin; Spider web © Yulia Glam; Santa © Pressmaster; Reindeer © Nejron Photo; Painted Easter eggs © leungchopan; Easter pattern © Mark Hall; Watermelon © Andrey Shtanko; Cupcakes © Ivonne Wierink; Hamburger © Sukharevskyy Dmytro (nevodka); Strawberries © DenisNata; Pineapple © Alex Staroseltsev; Graffiti © gudinny; Bunting © Ann Precious; Painted stones © Ungor; Stone pile © Mircea BEZERGHEANU; Dinosaur © Ken Benner; Frog © Tracie Andrews; Lion, Dog, Rhino, Cat © kvitka; Spider, Butterfly, Snail © Klara Viskova.

Contents

Rock Painting Origins

The earliest form of rock painting was cave painting. These prehistoric paintings were made on cave walls and ceilings. Many of these caves are located in areas that are not easily accessible. Scientists don't agree on what these early cave paintings mean. Some think that the paintings were a way for people to communicate with each other while others think that they had religious significance.

Many of these original cave paintings are of wild animals such as horses, deer and bison. The colors used in these early cave paintings were mostly red, brown, yellow and black.

It was also common to paint outlines of human hands on the cave walls. This was often done by holding a hand against the cave wall and then using a pipe made from bones to spray paint onto the cave wall, creating an outline of the hand.

Today, rock painting is a crafty hobby that many people enjoy. Painted rocks are used to decorate houses and gardens. They make a unique gift. Once you start rock painting, everyone is sure to enjoy your creations.

HUNDREDS OF PAINTINGS

In some caves, paintings were added until there were hundreds of different paintings by many different painters.

Rock Painting Timeline

ABOUT 40,000 YEARS AGO

Cave paintings were made in Australia, Spain and France

ABOUT 30,000 YEARS AGO

Cave paintings were made in parts of Africa

12,000 YEARS AGO

Cave paintings were made in India

2000 YEARS AGO

Cave paintings were made in Asia and North America

TODAY

Cave paintings are still being found that date back to prehistoric times

All About Rocks

The Earth is made of rocks and minerals. Inside the Earth there is a liquid core of molten rock and on the outside there is a hard crust. The crust is made up of rocks and minerals. Much of the crust is covered by water, sand, soil and ice. If you dig deep enough, you will always hit rock.

Rocks and Minerals

The rocks you see around you – the mountains, canyons and riverbanks – are all made of minerals. A rock is made up of two or more minerals. All rocks can be classified into three groups according to the way they were formed: igneous, sedimentary and metamorphic.

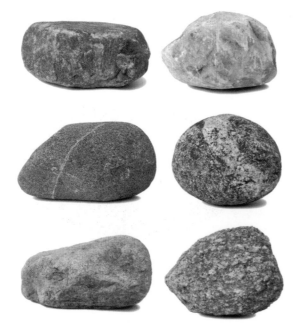

Igneous, Sedimentary and Metamorphic

Igneous rock forms when molten lava (magma) cools and turns to solid rock. The magma comes from the Earth's core. Sedimentary rocks are formed by the deposit of minerals, plants and other organic materials at the bottom of lakes and oceans. The sediment is compressed over a long time before fusing into solid layers of rock. Metamorphic rocks are rocks that have changed. Metamorphic rocks were originally igneous or sedimentary, but were changed by heat and pressure caused by movement of the Earth's crust.

The Rock Cycle

Rocks are constantly being formed, worn down and then formed again. This is known as the rock cycle. This cycle occurs slowly over millions of years. Over time, processes on the Earth such as erosion and water flow, change rocks from one form to another and then back again.

FAST FACT

Broken bits of shale tumble to the bottom of hills and riverbanks, where they are washed away by waves and water. When they are deposited at the side of rivers and on the beach, they are smooth. This is caused by abrasion while being transported in moving water.

Rock Collection

Ordinary river rocks and water tumbled stones are wonderful for rock painting. Whenever you are out walking, keep your eyes open for rocks to collect and bring home for painting. Even small pebbles can be painted!

Getting Started

Rock painting is a lot of fun but before you can jump in, there are some basic things you need to do to get everything ready.

Rocks to Work With

Do you sometimes get home from a walk or the beach with pockets full of rocks? Are there rocks scattered all over your bedroom? Yes? Then you've got lots of material to work with already!

Choose Carefully

It's important to choose the right rock for your planned design. Rocks come in lots of shapes and sizes and some are better for certain designs than others. Imagine how your sketch will look on the rock before you begin. If it doesn't work with the rock shape, choose another rock.

Set Up

Have your palette and all your paints, brushes and other materials ready before you start. You don't want to be disturbed by needing to find materials once you've started painting.

Outdoor Paint

If any of your rock painting creations are intended to live outdoors, make sure you use outdoor paint. It would be such a shame if all your hard work washed away in the next rainstorm. Outdoor craft paint can be bought from most craft stores.

TOP TIP
Painted rocks make great paperweights. To add a unique twist use magnetic paint and then your rocks can also be used to hold paperclips!

TOP TIP
Thin rocks can be placed in a bull clip and held so you can paint both sides of the rock. There's no time wasted waiting for one side to dry!

Clean and Tidy

Painting can be messy so make sure you always cover your work area with old newspaper and have an old cloth on hand to wipe up any paint spills. Wear an apron or old shirt to protect your clothes.

Rock Painting Techniques

It takes some planning and creativity to create rock paintings. Follow these simple techniques to make sure your rock paintings look fantastic and draw attention.

Sketch First

Always sketch out your plan before you lift a paintbrush. It's easier to envision what the finished project will look like if you draw it first with pencil on paper. You can then refer back to your sketch as you paint to help you stay on track.

Right Brush for the Right Job

There are different sizes and types of paintbrushes. Each paintbrush is useful in different ways. Fine paintbrushes with round ends are good for decorations, details, outlines and final touches. Larger flat paintbrushes are good for backgrounds, blends and flat washes.

Dry, Dry, Dry

Make sure you allow the rock to dry between each coat of paint and each newly painted detail. It's very easy to smudge wet paint. If it's a sunny day, leave the rock to dry in the sun. Always paint one side of the rock and allow it to dry before turning it to paint the other side.

Color Mixing

Primary colors are colors that no other color combination can produce. From the three primary colors – red, blue and yellow – it's possible to make nearly any color. This means that you only really need these color paints, plus white and black, for your rock painting. Here's a guide to simple color mixing.

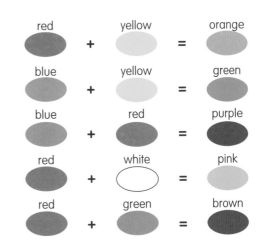

red	+	yellow	=	orange
blue	+	yellow	=	green
blue	+	red	=	purple
red	+	white	=	pink
red	+	green	=	brown

Finishing Spray

To protect your painted rock creations you can paint or spray a gloss (shiny) or matte (no shine) sealant on top. You can buy sealant from most craft stores.

Caring for your Brushes

Follow these simple rules of caring for your paintbrushes.
- Always clean your brushes between color changes.
- Never allow paint to dry on your brushes.
- Never let a brush sit in water. Clean or rinse your brushes and remove them from the water container. When the painting session is finished, clean all your brushes.
- Dry the brushes and reshape them with your fingers.
- Store your paintbrushes either lying flat or with the brush end upright.

Lovely Ladybug

Ladybugs are fun and easy to paint on rocks, and look great. A few of them placed in the garden look wonderful and brighten things up nicely. They also make sweet gifts for family or friends.

You will need:

- Red, black, blue and white paint
- A small round or oval rock
- A medium flat brush
- A small flat brush
- A small round brush
- Chalk
- Pencil
- Paper
- Felt circles (optional)

How to Paint a Ladybug

1 Select a rock. Small round or oval rocks are the best shape for ladybugs.

2 Paint the rock with a basecoat of white with a medium flat brush. Colors such as red or yellow look best and are brighter when painted on a white basecoat.

3 Once the white has dried, paint the rock red all over. You might need to give the rock two or three coats of red before you have solid coverage.

4 Sketch out a ladybug design on paper.

5 Refer to your sketch and use chalk to map out the area for the head, then draw a line down the center of the body.

TOP TIP
You don't have to use red as your base color for ladybugs. Yellow, pink, blue and even purple look good, too.

6 Paint the head black with the small flat brush. Paint the line down the body black with the small round brush.

7 Add black dots to the body. You can do this with a round brush or dip your finger in black paint and apply to the body. You could also use the base of a pen or pencil as a round stamp to apply the black paint dots.

8 With chalk, draw a line down the center of the face, dividing it in half. This will help you evenly draw in the eyes, nose and mouth. Use the chalk to draw a mouth.

9 To draw the eye outlines use a pencil, as chalk is too thick. You can outline felt circles or create circle templates by cutting circles out of thick paper. This will ensure your ladybug eyes are perfectly and evenly round.

10 Paint the inside of the eyes white with a small round brush. You might need to do more than one coat.

11 Paint two white nostril holes on either side of the chalk line running down the middle of the face.

12 Paint the chalk mouth line white with the small round brush or the thinnest brush you have.

13 Paint a smaller black circle inside each eye. You can use small felt circles or handmade circle templates to help with this.

14 Paint a small white dot within the black circles with the small round brush. Paint a blue outline around each black circle, slightly thicker at the top than the bottom.

15 Paint over the white mouth line in red with the small round brush.

16 Paint thin white arches above each eye for the antennae.

17 When dry, your ladybug rock painting is finished!

Terrific Turtle

A turtle shell is the perfect image to paint onto a rock. In this design, craft sticks form the turtle's legs and face and the painted rock is used to make the shell.

You will need:

- Green, black and brown paint
- A medium oval or round rock
- A medium flat brush
- A small flat brush
- A small round brush
- Chalk
- Pencil
- Paper
- 2 small googly eyes
- 3 craft sticks, 1 complete and 2 broken in half
- Craft or cement glue (ask an adult for help if using cement glue)

How to Paint a Turtle

1 Select a rock. Medium round or oval rocks are the best shape for turtle shells.

2 Paint the rock with green paint all over using a medium flat brush. If your green paint is too bright, mix it with some blue paint. You might need to give the rock two or three coats before you have solid coverage.

3 Paint the craft sticks all over using the same green paint and medium flat brush.

4 Sketch out a turtle shell design on paper.

5 Refer to your sketch and map out the sections of the turtle's shell on the rock using chalk.

6 Use craft glue to stick the four craft stick pieces to the complete craft stick as shown.

7 Use craft glue to stick the googly eyes to the top of the complete craft stick.

8 Paint the chalk shell outlines black with a small round brush.

9 Using the brown paint and the small flat brush, fill in the sections of the shell.

10 Glue the painted rock to the painted craft stick legs and face. Be sure to ask an adult for help if using cement glue.

11 When dry, your turtle rock painting is finished!

TOP TIP
Instead of using craft sticks for the turtle's face and legs you could use five small rocks. Paint toes on four of them and eyes on one and glue them underneath your painted shell rock.

Flashy Fish

Clown fish are bright and attractive. They live in coral reefs. You're sure to find a rock perfectly shaped to make a great clown fish rock painting.

You will need:

- Orange, white and black paint
- A small flat rock with a peak at the top
- A medium flat brush
- A small flat brush
- A small round brush
- Chalk
- Pencil
- Paper

How to Paint a Clown Fish

1 Select a rock. Small flat rocks with a peak at the top are the best shape for clown fish.

2 Paint the rock with a basecoat of white using a medium flat brush. Colors such as orange and yellow look best and are brighter when painted on a white basecoat.

3 Paint the rock with bright orange paint all over. You might need to give the rock two or three coats before you have solid coverage. If you don't have orange paint, you can make it by mixing yellow and red paint. Start with yellow paint and add a small amount of red paint to it very slowly. You won't need much red paint.

4 Sketch out a clown fish design on paper.

5 Refer to your sketch and map out the sections for the white stripes and fin on the rock using chalk.

6 Paint the stripes white using a small flat brush. You might need to paint two or three coats.

7 Paint black outlines around the white stripes using the small round brush. Keep your hand steady. Add extra definition to the fin with black paint.

8 Use a small round brush to paint a black dot for the eye and a small smile for the mouth.

9 When dry, your clown fish rock painting is finished!

TOP TIP
Clown fish live in coral reefs. Paint some rocks with coral to place around your clown fish so it's in its environment. Starfish are also fun to paint on rocks!

Cute Caterpillar

A series of painted rocks lined up in a row make a great caterpillar. You can even glue all the rocks together!

You will need:

- A selection of color paints
- Six or more similar-sized rocks
- A medium flat brush
- A small flat brush
- A small round brush
- Chalk
- Pencil
- Paper
- Craft or cement glue (optional – ask an adult for help if using cement glue)

How to Paint a Caterpillar

1   Select six or more rocks. Make sure they are similar sizes but choose smaller ones for the head rock and final rock.

2   Paint the rocks with a basecoat of white using a medium flat brush. Many colors are brighter when painted on a white basecoat.

3   Paint each rock a different color using a medium flat brush. Choose colors that complement each other.

4 Sketch out design patterns for each rock on paper. Choose a different design for each rock. Plan what color paints you will use for the details on each rock.

5 Refer to your sketch and use a small round brush or flat brush to paint dots, stripes and any other kind of designs you sketched for each rock. Use the color paints you used in your design.

6 Paint a face on the first rock.

7 Use a small round brush to paint little legs and feet on the sides of all the rocks except the head.

8 Place a large amount of glue between each rock and stick them together. Be sure to ask an adult for help if using cement glue.

9 When dry, your caterpillar rock painting is finished!

TOP TIP
Caterpillars turn into butterflies. Trace the butterfly design on page 48 and use it to paint a butterfly rock painting.

Buzzing Bee

Painted bee rocks look very cute and cheery. They are bright and happy and look great inside on a windowsill.

You will need:

- Yellow, black and white paint
- A round-, oval- or teardrop-shaped rock
- A medium flat brush
- A small round brush
- Chalk
- Pencil
- Paper

How to Paint a Bee

1 Select a rock. Round-, oval- or teardrop-shaped rocks are best for bees.

2 Paint the rock with a basecoat of white using a medium flat brush. Colors such as orange or yellow look best and are brighter when painted on a white basecoat.

3 Once the white has dried, paint the rock yellow all over with a flat brush. You might need to give the rock two or three coats of yellow before you have solid coverage.

4 Sketch out a bee design on paper.

5 Refer to your sketch and map out the stripes on the rock using chalk. You can make the stripes straight or wavy.

6 Paint over the chalk stripes with black paint using the small round brush. You can make the stripes as thick or as thin as you like.

7 With chalk, mark where each eye will go on the rock. Paint the eyes black using the small round brush. You can use the eraser end of a pencil to make the two eyes. Simply dip the eraser in black paint and stamp over the chalk circles. This will ensure your bee eyes are perfectly and evenly round.

8 Paint a white antenna above each eye with the small round brush. Keep a steady hand.

9 Using the small round brush, paint a black circle for the nose. Add a curved line for the mouth.

10 Add a small white dot to each eye. You can use the end of a thin paintbrush to do this.

11 Use chalk to sketch the wings onto the rock.

12 Use the small round brush to paint the outline of the wings in white paint.

13 When dry, your bee rock painting is finished!

TOP TIP
If you want to paint the bee's wings, dilute white paint with water to make it transparent. It needs to be thin enough that you can see the bee's yellow body through the paint. Use a small flat brush to lightly paint the outline of the wings.

Outstanding Owl

Owls are great subjects for rock paintings. You can make your painted owl rock look adorable by using pastel colors.

You will need:

- Green, beige, white, yellow and black paint
- An oval flat rock
- A medium flat brush
- A small flat brush
- A small round brush
- Chalk
- Pencil
- Paper

How to Paint an Owl

1 Select a rock. Oval rocks are the best shape for owls.

2 Paint the rock with a basecoat of white using a medium flat brush.

3 Once the white has dried, paint the rock beige all over with a small or medium flat brush. You might need to give the rock two or three coats of beige before you have solid coverage. If you don't have beige paint, mix some red and yellow paint and add a dash of blue. Mix a small amount of this with some white paint. Keep adding the color mix until you have a warm beige color.

4 Sketch out an owl design on paper.

5 Refer to your sketch and map out the outline of the owl's wings, body and face on the rock in chalk (use colored chalk if it's hard to see white chalk on the beige).

6 Use the small flat brush to paint the wings light green. Lighten your green paint by adding some white paint. This makes a warmer pastel color.

7 Use the small round brush to paint around the face with blue paint.

8 With the small round brush, paint large white ovals for the eyes.

9 With the small round brush paint a small yellow upside-down triangle shape for the nose.

10 With the end of a fine paintbrush paint small blue dots onto the owl's chest.

11 With the end of a fine paintbrush add a black dot to the inside of both eyes.

12 When dry, your owl rock painting is finished!

TOP TIP

You don't always have to paint the whole animal's body on the rock. You could just do the face. Owls have very interesting eyes so you could make this a focus of your rock painting.

Perfect Panda

Create a complete panda rock painting by stacking multiple rocks on top of each other. Each rock has a certain part of the panda's body painted on it. The result looks adorable.

You will need:

- Black, white and pink paint
- A large round rock with a flat bottom, an oval flat rock, two small black pebbles
- A medium flat brush
- A small flat brush
- A small round brush
- Chalk
- Pencil
- Paper
- Black felt tip pen
- Craft or cement glue (ask an adult for help if using cement glue)

How to Paint a Panda

1 Select your rocks. The large round rock will need to be able to rest securely on its flat bottom. The oval flat rock will be glued to the large round rock so make sure they connect. The two small black pebbles will be stuck to the flat rock for the panda's ears.

2 Paint the large round rock and the oval flat rock white using a medium flat brush. You might need to give the rocks two or three coats of white before you have solid coverage.

TOP TIP
Gluing rocks together can be tricky. In addition to cement glue, there are hot glues that will ensure your rocks remain stuck. Be sure to ask an adult for help with hot glues.

3 Sketch out a panda design for each rock on paper. The large rock is for the belly and needs to include the panda's arms and belly button. The oval flat rock is for the panda's face.

4 Refer to your sketch and use chalk to map out the outline of the panda's belly on the large rock.

5 Use the small flat brush to paint the panda's black arms and belly base.

6 Use a black felt tip pen or small round brush to add a belly button in black paint.

7 Refer to your sketch and use pencil to draw where the eyes, nose and mouth will go on the flat rock.

8 Using the small round brush, paint large black ovals for the eyes.

9 Using the small round brush, paint a small pink oval shape for the nose.

10 With the end of a fine paintbrush add a white dot to the inside of both eyes.

11 Use a black felt tip pen or small round brush to add a small smile.

12 Glue the oval flat rock to the large round rock. Be sure to ask an adult for help if using cement glue.

13 Glue the two small black pebbles to the oval flat rock as ears. Be sure to ask an adult for help if using cement glue.

14 When dry, your panda rock painting is finished!

Ghostly Ghoul

Did you ever think a rock could look scary? It will once you've painted this ghostly ghoul!

You will need:

- Black, white and bright green paint
- A large flat rock
- A medium flat brush
- A small flat brush
- A small round brush
- Chalk
- Pencil
- Paper
- Black felt tip pen

How to Paint a Ghost

1 Select your rock. A large flat rock works best for painting a ghoulish ghost.

2 Paint the rock white using a medium flat brush. This is a basecoat and will make sure the bright green is as bright and ghoulish as possible.

3 Paint the rock green all over using a medium flat brush. Apply a second green coat so the color is really bright.

4 Sketch out a ghost design on paper. Look at the ghost faces on the next page for some ideas for extra detail.

5 Refer to your sketch and use chalk to map out the outline of the ghost on the rock.

6 With the small flat brush, paint the interior of the ghost white.

7 Use the small round brush to outline the ghost in black paint. This needs a steady hand, so take your time.

8 Use the small round brush to paint in the black dots for eyes and an open mouth. Use a black felt tip pen if your face design is more detailed.

9 When dry, your ghost rock painting is finished!

TOP TIP
You can paint large heavy rocks as simple ghosts. The unusual shapes of these rocks look really good as ghosts. Paint the whole rock white (two coats should be enough) and then paint two black oval eyes and a black round nose on the front of the rock. Simple and fun!

Some ghost face design ideas.

Jazzy Jack-o'-Lantern

Painted rocks make great Halloween decorations. Round flat rocks are the perfect shape for jack-o'-lanterns. It looks great to have several of these grouped together, all with slightly different facial expressions.

You will need:

- Orange, black, white and green paint
- An oval or round flat rock
- A medium flat brush
- A small round brush
- Chalk
- Pencil
- Paper

How to Paint a Jack-o'-Lantern

1 Select your rock. A flat oval or round rock works best for painting a jack-o'-lantern.

2 Paint the rock with a basecoat of white using a medium flat brush.

3 Paint the rock orange all over using a medium flat brush. Apply a second orange coat so the color is bright and you have good coverage. If you don't have orange paint, you can make it by mixing yellow and red paint. Start with yellow paint and add red to it very slowly. You won't need much red paint.

4 Sketch out a jack-o'-lantern design on paper. Look at the jack-o'-lantern faces at the bottom of these pages for some ideas for extra detail.

5 Refer to your sketch and use chalk to map out the outline of the jack-o'-lantern on the rock.

6 Using the small round brush paint the jack-o'-lantern's eyes, nose and mouth with black paint.

TOP TIP

Can't choose which expression to use? Don't just make one jack-o'-lantern rock painting, make 10! These rocks look great when there are lots of them, all with different features and expressions.

7 Use the small round brush to paint a small green stem at the top.

8 When dry, your jack-o'-lantern rock painting is finished!

Some jack-o'-lantern design ideas.

Spooky Spider

Having a spooky spider rock painting on your window ledge is much cuter than having a real spider! The black pipe cleaners form the spider's hairy legs and the painted rock is the spider's body.

You will need:

- Black, gray and white paint
- An oval or round rock
- A medium flat brush
- A small round brush
- Chalk
- Pencil
- Paper
- 4 black pipe cleaners
- Craft glue

How to Paint a Spider

1 Select your rock. An oval or round rock works best for painting a spider.

2 Paint the rock with a basecoat of white using a medium flat brush.

3 Paint the rock black all over using a medium flat brush. Apply a second black coat so you have good coverage.

4 Sketch out a design on paper for the face of your spider.

5 Refer to your sketch and use chalk to map out where the eyes and mouth are to go on the rock.

6 You can add hairy detail to the spider's body using a small round brush and gray paint.

7 Fold each black pipe cleaner in half. Glue two folded pipe cleaners on the bottom of each side of the rock to form the spider's eight legs.

8 Using the small round brush paint the spider's mouth with white paint.

9 Using the small round brush paint the eyes white. When dry, add a small black dot to each eye.

10 When dry, your spider rock painting is finished!

TOP TIP
Why not paint another rock with a spider web to sit next to your spooky spider rock painting?

Super Santa

Rock paintings make unique and special Christmas decorations. Round and oval rocks work best for Santa's face. The longer the rock, the bushier Santa's beard will be!

You will need:

- Black, white, red, blue and pink paint
- An oval or round flat rock
- A medium flat brush
- A small round brush
- Chalk (colored)
- Pencil
- Paper
- Black paint pen or felt tip pen
- Glitter

How to Paint Santa

1   Select your rock. A flat oval or round rock works best for painting a Santa face.

2   Paint the rock with a basecoat of white using a medium flat brush.

3   Paint another coat of white all over the rock using a medium flat brush.

4   Sketch out a Santa face design on paper. Look at the Santa face here for an idea of the features you could include.

5 Refer to your sketch and use colored chalk or pencil to map out the outline of Santa's hat, beard, eyes, nose and mouth on the rock.

6 Paint Santa's hat red using the medium flat brush.

7 Use the small round brush to outline the white sections of Santa's hat with black paint. For a finer line use a paint pen or felt tip pen.

8 Use the small round brush to paint Santa's face a skin tone. Mix pink paint with white paint until you have a natural skin color.

9 Use the small round brush to outline Santa's nose, eyes and mouth with black paint. For a finer line use a paint pen or felt tip pen.

10 Use the small round brush to fill in Santa's eyebrows, eyes and moustache with white paint. Using the same brush, add some red paint to Santa's mouth and cheeks.

11 Use the small round brush to add some texture and detail to Santa's white beard. You could add some tone by mixing a small amount of blue paint in with some white paint and painting long stripes down Santa's beard area.

12 While the paint is still wet, sprinkle some glitter onto Santa's beard. It will stick to the paint and add sparkle.

13 When dry, your Santa rock painting is finished!

TOP TIP
Glue a looped ribbon to the top of your painted rock and hang it on your Christmas tree as a new and unique ornament!

Radical Reindeer

It's up to you whether or not you give your reindeer a red nose. You could even create a rock painting for each of Santa's reindeer – Dasher, Dancer, Prancer, Vixen, Comet, Cupid, Donner, Blitzen and Rudolph, of course!

You will need:

- Black, white, brown and red paint
- A slightly oval flat rock
- A medium flat brush
- A small round brush
- Chalk
- Pencil
- Paper
- 2 twigs (optional)

How to Paint a Reindeer

1 Select your rock. A slightly oval rock works best for painting a reindeer head.

2 Paint the rock with a basecoat of white using a medium flat brush.

3 Paint a coat of brown all over the rock using a medium flat brush. Apply a second coat to ensure you have good coverage.

4 Sketch out a reindeer face design on paper. One option is to make the head section round with a small oval overlapping at the bottom of it. Two pointy ears on either side of the head and the antlers are all that need to be added (if you're not using twigs for antlers).

5 Refer to your sketch and use chalk to map out the outline of the reindeer's face on the rock. It might make it easier to think of the shapes within the design.

6 Use the small round brush to paint the chalked face outline in white on the rock.

7 Use the small round brush to paint the eyes.

8 With the end of a fine paintbrush add a black dot to the inside of both eyes.

9 Use the small round brush to paint the ears black.

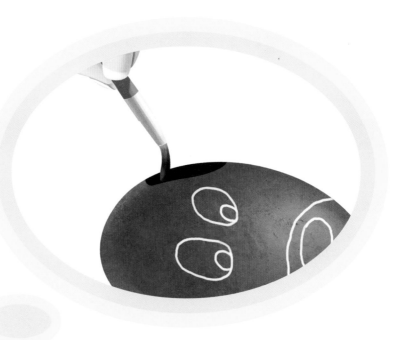

10 Use the small round brush to paint the reindeer's nose red (optional).

11 If using, glue the twigs to the top of the rock at the back to act as the antlers.

12 When dry, your reindeer rock painting is finished!

TOP TIP
You can add fine texture to the reindeer's fur with a liner brush and some white paint. Make sure you follow the direction of the fur and paint small white lines.

Excellent Easter Egg

In addition to painting real eggs, painted rock eggs make lovely Easter decorations. You can even use them in your Easter egg hunt along with the chocolate ones!

You will need:

- A selection of pastel-colored paints or metallic paint if you have it
- White paint
- An oval rock
- A medium flat brush
- A small round brush
- Chalk
- Pencil
- Paper
- Glitter

How to Paint an Easter Egg

1 Select your rock. An oval-shaped rock works best for painting an Easter egg.

2 Paint the rock with a basecoat of white using a medium flat brush.

3 Paint the rock a pastel color all over using a medium flat brush. Apply a second coat so you have good coverage. If you don't have any pastel-colored paints you can lighten your bright color paints by adding white or yellow paint. Metallic paint also looks good if you have it.

4 Sketch out an Easter pattern on paper. Look at the patterns below for inspiration. You can use a combination of dots, zigzags and stripes, for example.

5 You can either treat the entire rock as the egg or paint an outline of an egg onto one side of the rock. Both look festive so it's up to you. Refer to your sketch and use chalk to map out the outline of the Easter patterns on the rock.

6 If you have chosen to outline the egg on the rock, use the small round brush to paint the outline of the egg in white.

7 With the small round brush, paint the patterns onto the rock, using different-colored paints for each pattern. Use the end of a fine paintbrush dipped in paint to add any dots.

8 When dry, your Easter egg rock painting is finished!

TOP TIP
A collection of painted rock Easter eggs look great in a cane basket full of straw (use shredded paper if you don't have any straw).

Some patterns for you to use as inspiration when painting your rock Easter egg.

Wonderful Watermelon

There's something particularly cute about rocks painted as food. Some rocks are perfectly shaped watermelon slices – look out for them for this design.

You will need:

- Red, black, white and green paint
- A curved triangular-shaped rock
- A medium flat brush
- A small round brush
- Chalk
- Pencil
- Paper

How to Paint a Watermelon

1 Select your rock. A curved triangular-shaped flat rock works best for painting a watermelon slice.

2 Paint the rock with a basecoat of white using a medium flat brush. Colors such as red or yellow look best and are brighter when painted on a white basecoat.

3 Once the white has dried, paint the rock red all over. You might need to give the rock two or three coats of red before you have solid coverage.

4 Sketch out a watermelon slice design on paper.

5 Refer to your sketch and use chalk to map out on the rock the sections for the red part of the fruit and the green rind. Think about how you want to place the seeds – scattered or in an arc.

6 Use the medium flat brush to paint the rind section green. This might take two coats to get good coverage.

7 Use the small round brush to paint a white line to separate the red section from the green rind. Add some wiggly white lines to the green rind section using the small round brush.

8 Paint teardrop-shaped seeds onto the red section as designed in your sketch. The seeds can be black, white or a combination. If teardrop shapes are too hard to create, just dab the paint on with your brush.

9 When dry, your watermelon rock painting is finished!

TOP TIP
As you get more confident painting on rocks you can think more about ways to add texture and detail to your paintings. You can also experiment with color mixing to create a whole new palette for your rock painting creations.

Cute Cupcake

Everyone loves cupcakes. But make sure you don't bite into this rock art creation – you might break a tooth!

You will need:

- A selection of pastel-colored paints
- A large round arched rock
- A medium flat brush
- A small round brush
- Chalk
- Pencil
- Paper

How to Paint a Cupcake

1 Select your rock. A large arch-topped rock works best for painting a cupcake. Try to find a rock that's about the size of an actual cupcake.

2 Paint the rock with a basecoat of white using a medium flat brush. Pastel colors look best and are brighter when painted on a white basecoat.

3 Sketch out a cupcake design on paper. Does your cupcake have a liner? If so, what color is it? Does it have a pattern on it? Then think about the cupcake. What color is the icing? Are there sprinkles? A cherry?

4 Once the white has dried, paint a pastel color of your choice all over. This should be the color of your cupcake liner or the color of the cupcake – yellow for vanilla or brown for chocolate. You might need to give the rock two or three coats before you have solid coverage.

5 Refer to your design and sketch the cupcake shape onto the rock using chalk. Show where the various toppings and decorations are to be painted.

6 Use the medium flat brush to paint the icing color onto the top section of the rock.

TOP TIP

Use a hole puncher to punch small circles of colored paper. Sprinkle these on top of your cupcake before the icing paint dries. The colored paper will look like round sprinkles.

7 Use the small round brush to paint on all the toppings and decorations.

8 When dry, your cupcake rock painting is finished!

Perfect Pizza

Transform a rock into a piping-hot slice of pizza. All you have to do is find the right shape rock and choose your toppings.

You will need:

- White, brown, green, red, black and yellow paint
- A flat triangular (isosceles) rock
- A medium flat brush
- A small round brush
- Chalk
- Pencil
- Paper

How to Paint a Pizza Slice

1 Select your rock. Think about a slice of pizza. It's an isosceles triangle shape, with two long sides and one short side (the crust).

2 Paint the rock with a basecoat of white using a medium flat brush.

3 Sketch out a pizza slice design on paper. Think about the toppings. Are there mushrooms? Ham? Black olives? Tomatoes?

4 Use chalk to sketch out where the crust is and where you want to place your various toppings on the rock.

5 Use the medium flat brush to paint a light-brown color for the crust section. Add some white paint to your brown paint if it's too dark.

6 Use your small round brush to paint your toppings. Try to make your paintings look like the vegetable or meat you're painting.

7 Use the small round brush to add some yellow sections for the melted cheese.

8 Use the small round brush to paint a brown outline around the toppings section of the rock. This adds definition to the rock.

9 When dry, your pizza slice rock painting is finished!

TOP TIP
Once you've mastered painting pizza-slice rocks, your next challenge is painting a hamburger rock. Find a rock that's the shape of a hamburger and focus on the colored layers of filling on the side.

Special Strawberry

Fresh strawberries are delicious in summer. With these rock paintings you'll be able to look at fresh strawberries all year round.

You will need:

- White, red, green and black paint
- A small oval rock
- A medium flat brush
- A small round brush
- A liner brush
- Chalk
- Pencil
- Paper

How to Paint a Strawberry

1 Select a rock. Small oval-shaped rocks are the best shape for strawberries. Try to find a rock that is about the same size and shape as a strawberry.

2 Paint the rock with a basecoat of white using a medium flat brush. Colors such as red look best and are brighter when painted on a white basecoat.

3 Once the white has dried, paint the rock red all over. You might need to give the rock two or three coats of red before you have solid coverage.

4 Sketch out a strawberry design on paper.

5 Refer to your sketch and use chalk to map out on the rock the section for the green hull. Place the hull on the less pointed end of the rock.

6 Use your small round brush to paint the green hull and leaves.

7 With your small round brush, use a darker green paint (add black to your green paint to darken it) to paint an outline around the hull and leaves. Add some texture and details to the leaves.

8 Use a small round brush to add small black lines for the strawberry seeds to the red section of the rock.

TOP TIP
It's easy to adapt these instructions to make pineapple rock paintings.

9 Use a liner brush to add tiny white dots to the black seed lines.

10 When dry, your strawberry rock painting is finished!

More Ideas

The only limit to what you can paint on rocks is your imagination. Don't feel you always have to paint specific objects – get your paints and rocks out and see what happens.

Words

Personalize a rock painting gift with words. Two rocks painted with the words 'Best Friends' make a lovely gift. You can also paint single letters on each rock to spell out words such as 'Home', 'Garden' or a person's name. Your unique and personal creation is sure to be appreciated.

Graffiti-inspired lettering looks great on rocks.

A row of rocks all painted with bunting looks gorgeous and is a great gift when a baby is born.

Patterns

Patterns look great painted on rocks. Create your own patterns and have fun painting them. If the end result turns out differently to what you had in mind that's okay. It's fun to just relax and paint patterns using different colors. When grouped together, patterned rocks make great decorations on windowsills or in the garden.

Rock Monsters

Painting rock monsters is lots of fun. Make rock monsters for your friends. Just paint rocks different colors and paint funny monster mouths and teeth on each. Add crazy eyes, or glue on googly ones, and they're ready to give away.

Let the Rock Decide

Sometimes the shape of a rock will bring an object to mind. This makes it a perfect rock to paint that object on! It's already the right shape and has already made you think of something specific.

Your Creations

Rock painting is a fun and relaxing creative hobby. The results are unique and handmade by YOU! Be sure to add your initials to the backs (or bottoms) of your rock painting creations and the year you painted them.

Patterns

Here are some images for tracing onto rocks and painting.